VERY FIRST ETUDES

(24 MINIATURES)

Built on elementary pianistic patterns for supplementary use
with any preparatory grade book

BY
JOHN THOMPSON

ISBN 978-1-70511-107-9

EXCLUSIVELY DISTRIBUTED BY

WILLIS MUSIC

HAL•LEONARD®

Visit Hal Leonard Online at
www.halleonard.com

Contact us:
Hal Leonard
7777 West Bluemound Road
Milwaukee, WI 53213
Email: info@halleonard.com

In Europe, contact:
Hal Leonard Europe Limited
42 Wigmore Street
Marylebone, London, W1U 2RN
Email: info@halleonardeurope.com

In Australia, contact:
Hal Leonard Australia Pty. Ltd.
4 Lentara Court
Cheltenham, Victoria, 3192 Australia
Email: info@halleonard.com.au

PREFACE

Etudes in the Preparatory Grade serve several purposes.

In addition to general technical development, they also provide much
needed practice in Reading — since, particularly in this early grade, each new
page is a new experience in note-reading.

Also, by repeating in various octaves on the piano pianistic figures already
learned in the Grade Book, the pupil is enabled to explore and become
acquainted with a larger area of the keyboard than can be safely covered in the
regular lesson material.

Only elementary figures have been employed and the author has con-
stantly kept in mind that even "exercises" must be tuneful in order to hold
the beginner's interest.

No tempo indications are given, as speed, after all, is comparative and
is better judged by the teacher for each pupil individually.

The addition of these VERY FIRST ETUDES to the regular lesson assign-
ment should better prepare the pupil for advancement to a First Grade Book.

John Thompson

CONTENTS

Play this as smoothly as possible. Avoid the effect of a "break" when the melody changes hands. Try to make it sound as if played with one hand.

No. 1

Here you have broken chords played staccato alternating with five-finger legato groups.
Make as much contrast as you can.

Don't forget to play with your best possible Hand Position.

No. 2

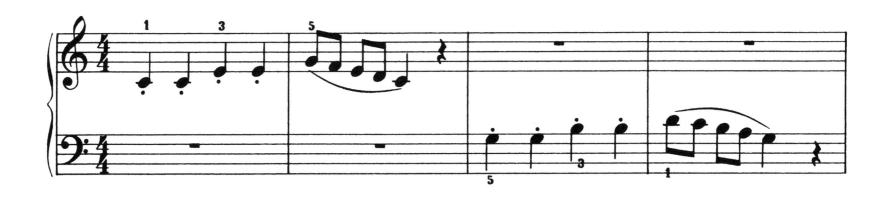

Another alternating legato and staccato – but this time the broken chords are played legato.

Are you watching your Hand Position?

No. 3

No. 4

Legato groups in Cross-Hand playing. See how gracefully you can pass the right hand over the left in measure 5.

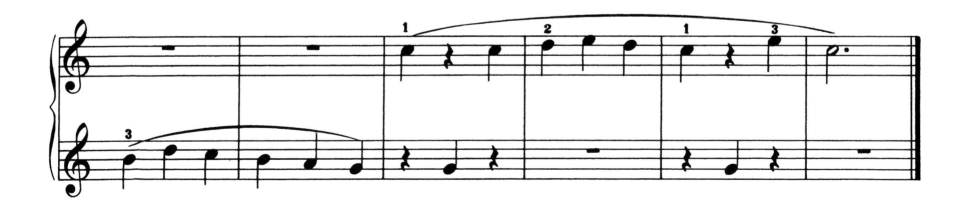

Five - finger legato groups divided between the hands.

A fine chance to display a good Hand Position and clean finger action.

No. 5

No. 6

Broken chords divided
between the hands
and played legato.

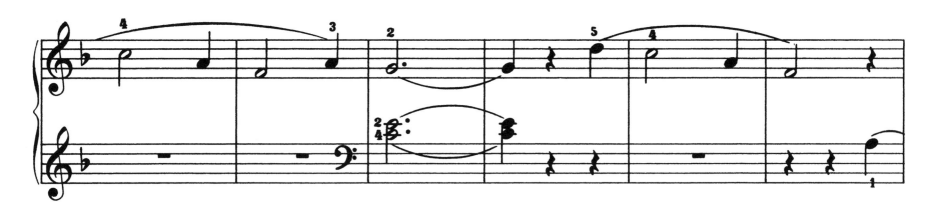

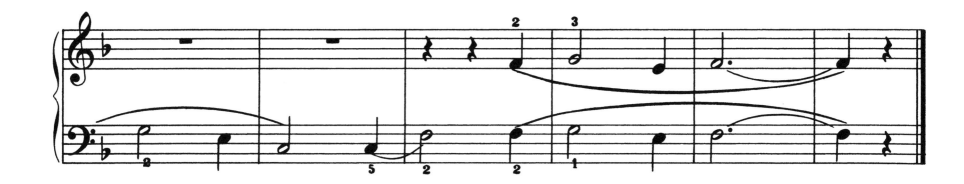

Trill figures ending with a staccato note.

No. 7

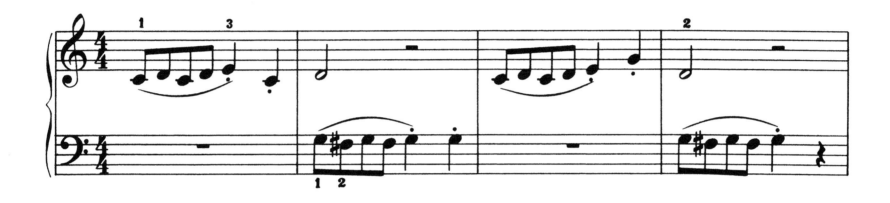

No. 8

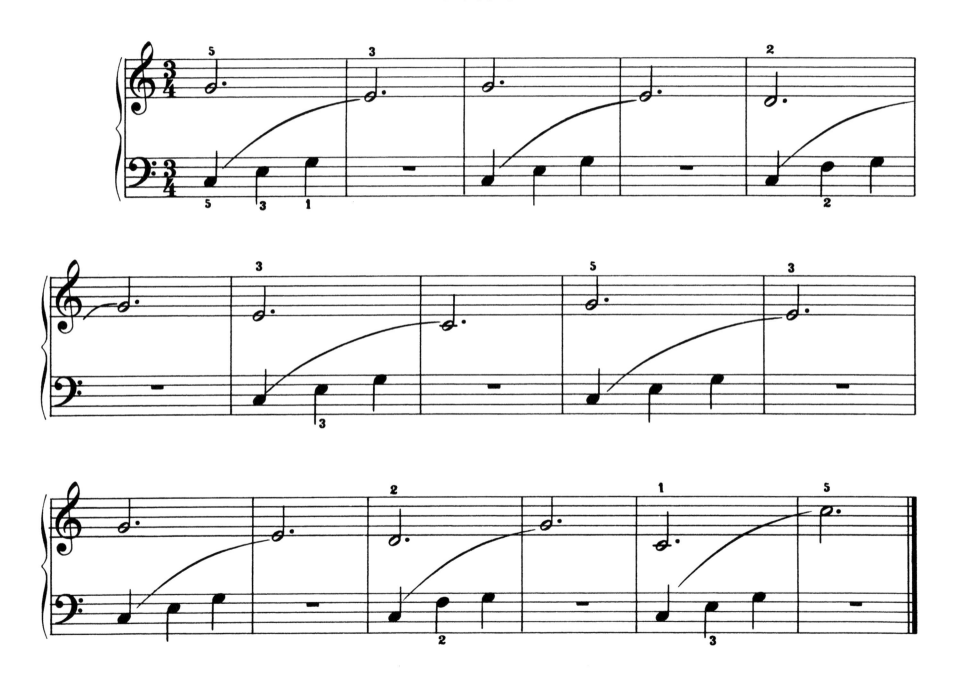

No. 9

"Jingle Bells" makes a fine Etude in staccato playing.

No. 10

Legato scale figures divided between the hands, alternating with sharp staccato quarter notes.

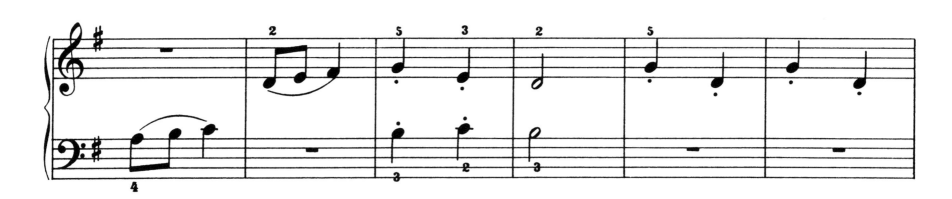

No. 11

The Bugle Call (Reveille) makes an Etude on Broken Chords.

No. 12

Adapted from "The Skaters" - Waldteufel

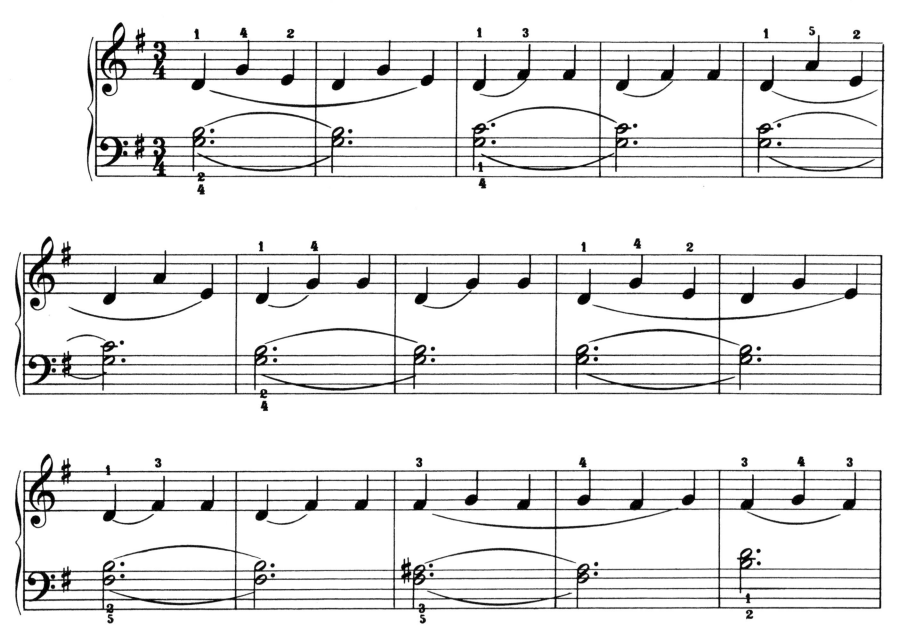

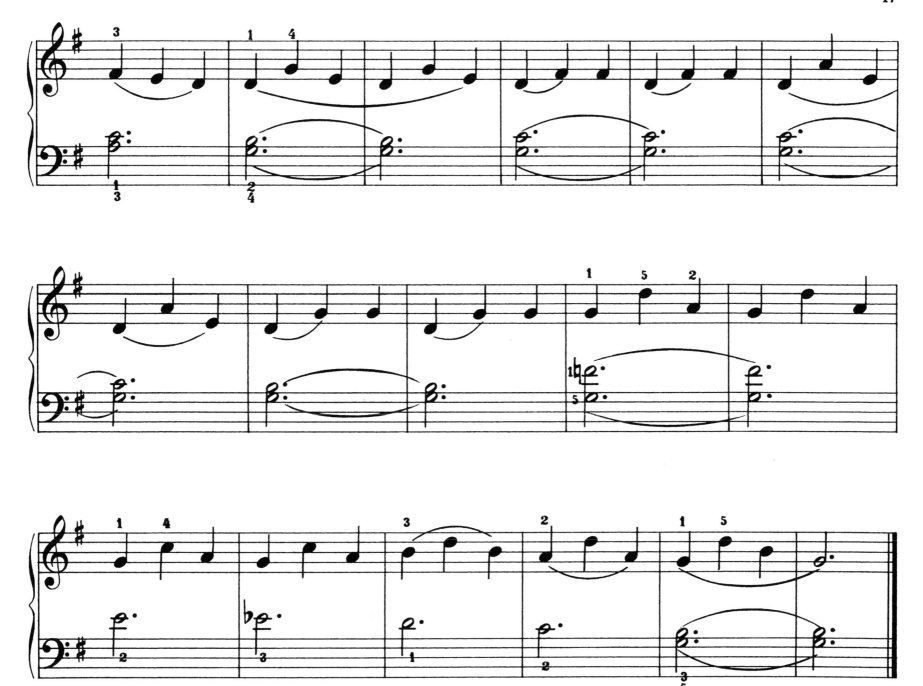

18

No. 13

A staccato note followed by three-finger legato groups. All to be played against a sustained left hand.

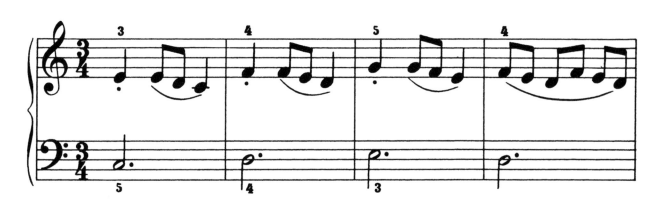

No. 14

In the style of an Irish Jig

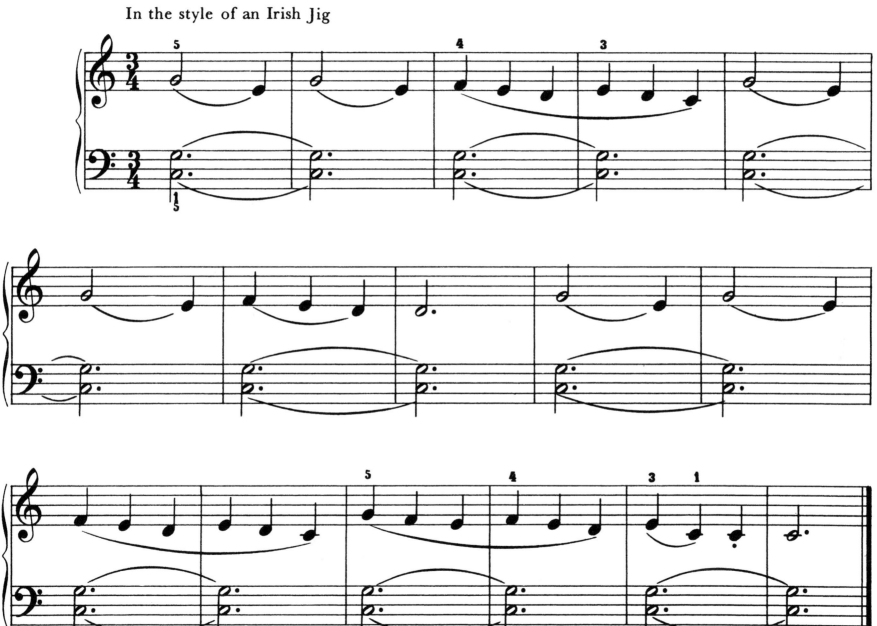

20

No. 15

An Etude on Chords.
There are only two simple
chords used in this example.

Learn to make the small
change from one to the other
and the rest will be simple.

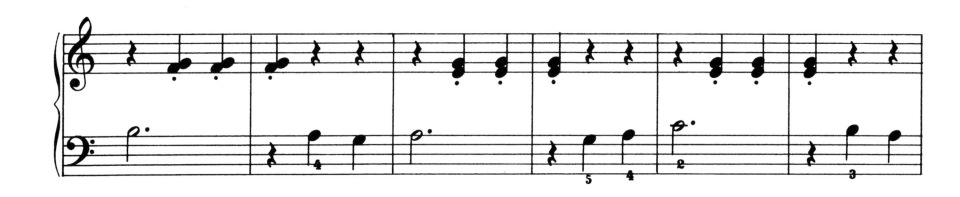

No. 16

Interlocking staccato is always lots of fun to play.

Learn to do it smoothly and thrill your friends with your dexterity.

No. 17

No. 18

It will be found very helpful to practice each hand separately – always a wise procedure.

The staccatos in one hand should be played against sustained chords in the other.

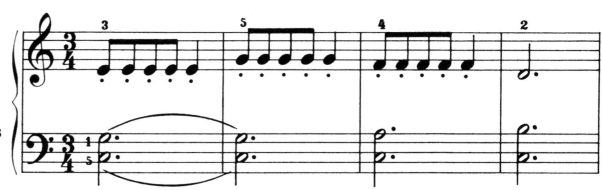

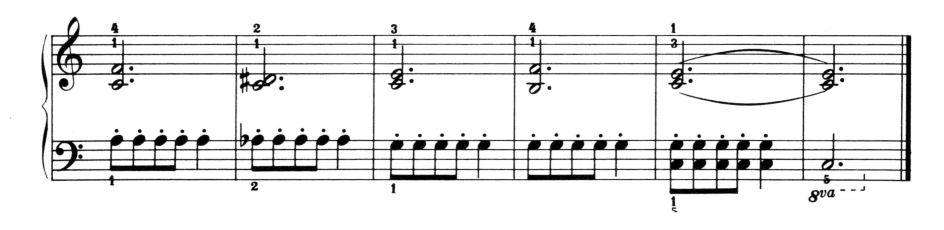

No. 19

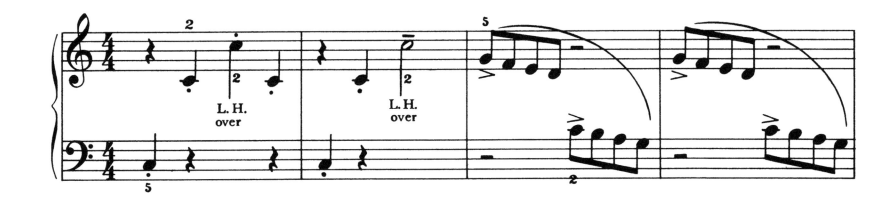

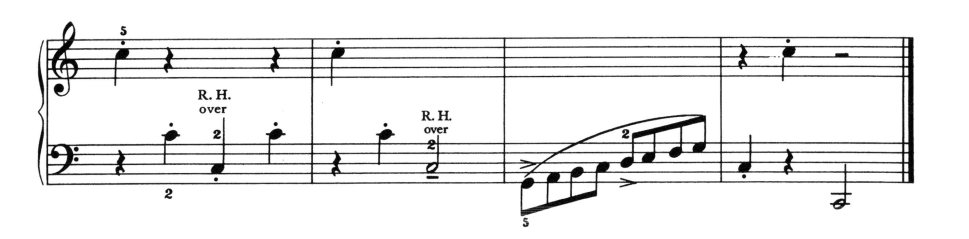

No. 20

Play the left hand staccato
with a heavy accent on the
first beat of each measure.

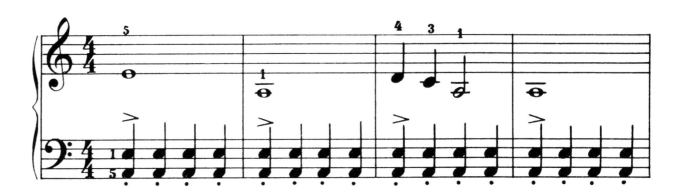

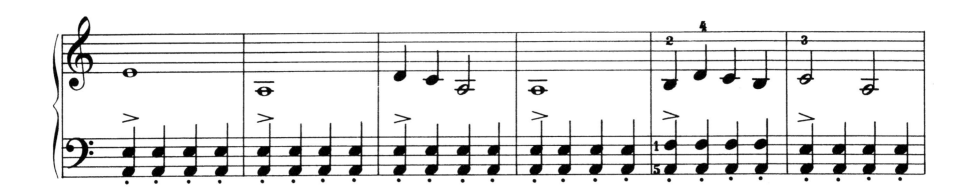

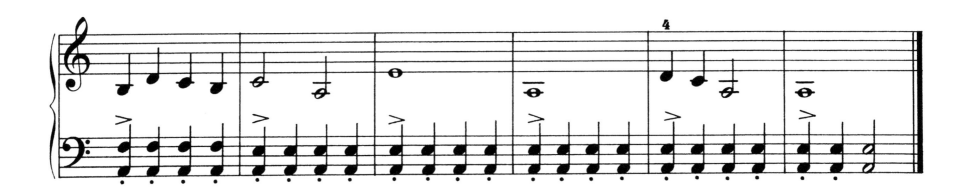

No. 21

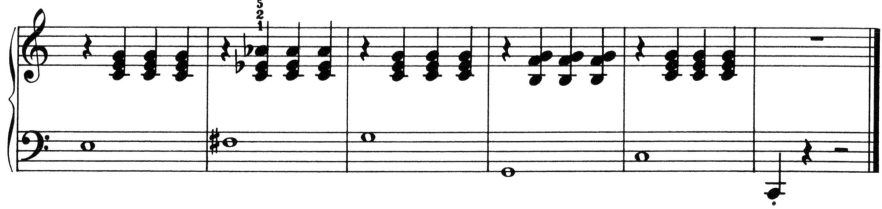

This etude is built on the Bohemian Song from the famous Opera, "Carmen", by Georges Bizet.

Be sure to apply sharp accents as marked in every other measure of the right hand.

No. 22

This is an adaption of the popular Chopin Prelude in C minor.
Some day you may play the original.
Meantime you can get real pleasure from this arrangement,
made for your special benefit.

No. 23

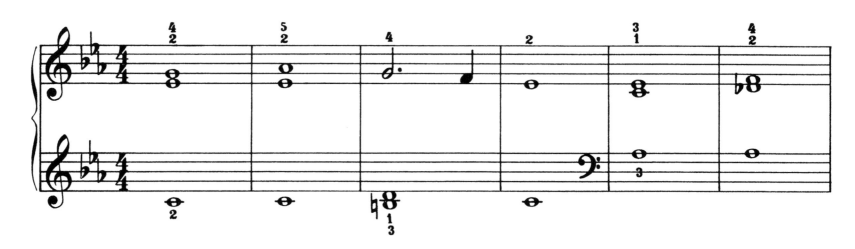

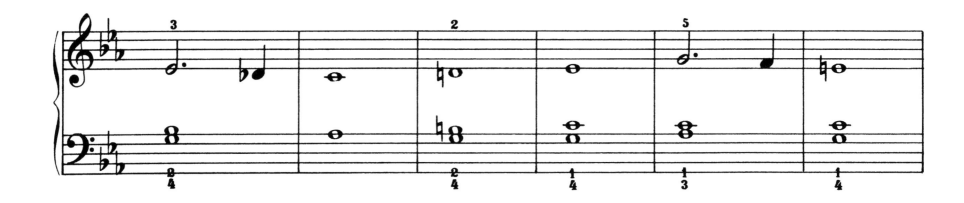

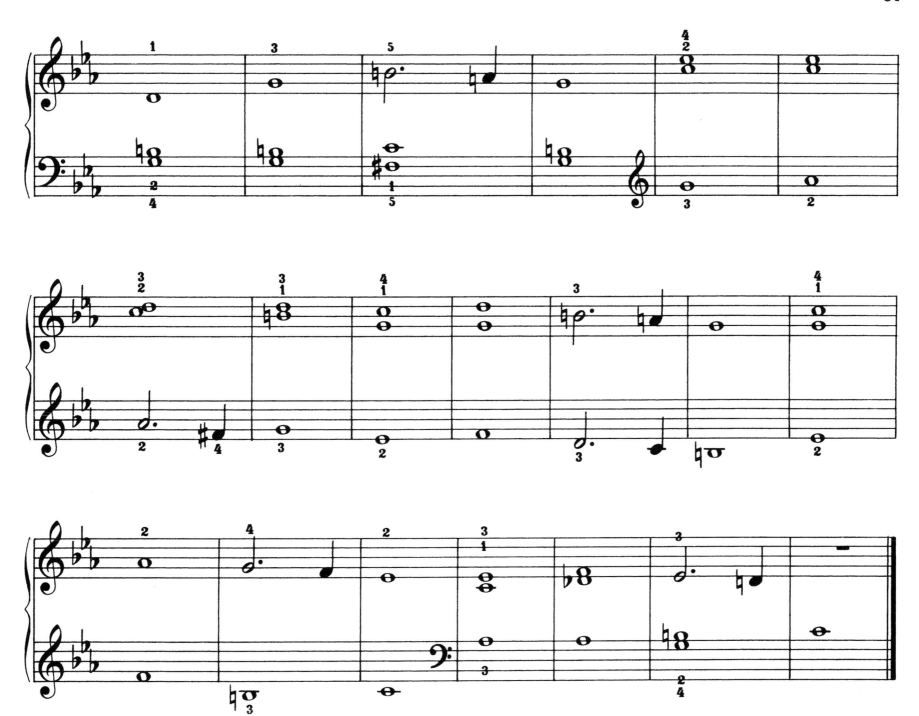

This last Etude presents an interesting chord Progression which you should memorize and try to transpose to other keys.

No. 24

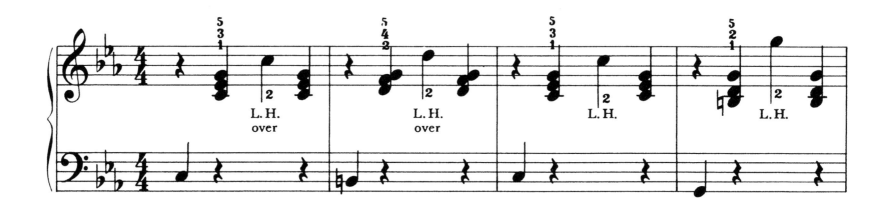

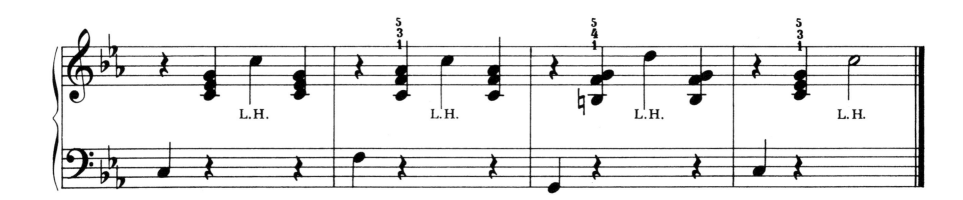